You Had Me At Topography

You Had Me At Topography

POEMS

Jessica Lakritz

Copyright © 2016 by Jessica Lakritz
All rights reserved.

Printed in the United States of America

Cover art: custom-made by Eilish Claire © 2016

Accompanying soundtrack: custom-made by Omar CT © 2016

Manufacturing by IngramSpark
Book Design by Jessica & Jessica LLC

First Printing, 2016

ISBN 978-0-9982766-0-1

For Luna

There are two ways to read this story.

1. Start at the first poem, and read through to the end, following the pages in numerical order.

2. Follow the page numbers at the end of each poem.

***

This book also includes a custom soundtrack,
meant to add a layer of ambiance and understanding
to the story in these poems, much as it would for a film.

You can find it at
jessicalakritz.com/youhadmeattopography

Contents [i]

One

A Different Angle • 5
You Were the Equator • 6
Lullaby • 7
Topography is All Surface • 8
This is love, not geology • 12
The Physical Things • 13
Suicide • 16
Safe • 18
Home Remedies • 20
With Regard to Sunsets • 22

Two

Buenos Aires, 2011 • 27
28 Reasons to Set My Furniture on Fire • 29
Math • 32
We find an empty part of the river • 35
Suspension • 37
This is geology, not love • 38
Pier 26 at Half Moon Bay • 41
The House of Sixteen Doors • 43
What Was Left • 45
The Midwest • 48
Buenos Aires, 2011 • 50

Three

An Incomplete List of Everything • 55
Elk Public House, 1:37am • 57
OkCupid • 59
Research • 60
Craving a Burrito at a Market, San Telmo, Buenos Aires • 61
Dear Mike Polansky, • 63
Chemistry on Hold • 64
Interrupted by the Infinite, in a Field
    or a Train or a Dream or • 67
The Graveyard's in the Backyard, Where
    the Meadow Used to Be • 71

Contents [ii]

A Different Angle • 5
Math • 32
OkCupid • 59
28 Reasons to Set My Furniture on Fire • 29
Suspension • 37
Buenos Aires, 2011 • 50
Craving a Burrito at a Market, San Telmo, Buenos Aires • 61
The Midwest • 48
Safe • 18
Elk Public House, 1:37am • 57
This is geology, not love • 38
Topography is All Surface • 8
The Graveyard's in the Backyard, Where
    the Meadow Used to Be • 71
With Regard to Sunsets • 22
Suicide • 16
An Incomplete List of Everything • 55
The Physical Things • 13
Pier 26 at Half Moon Bay • 41
Home Remedies • 20
Lullaby • 7
What Was Left • 45
Research • 60
Interrupted by the Infinite, in a Field
    or a Train or a Dream or • 67
Buenos Aires, 2011 • 27
Chemistry on Hold • 64

You Were the Equator • 6
Dear Mike Polansky, • 63
This is love, not geology • 12
We find an empty part of the river • 35
The House of Sixteen Doors • 43

You Had Me At Topography

One

A Different Angle

Take the ocean, take love—as if
just like that, I'm watching it wash up
over sea glass and busted shells. Take
intimacy, collecting
tiny Redwood cones, a lunar eclipse we'd
accidentally seen, coincidence and once-in-a-
few-hundred-years events that enter and exit
in silence, leave us feeling enormous
and insignificant. The plans, the placebos,
the excuses, miniscule or not, drift in and out
as if part of a dream, then land like earth-
quakes, spitting up dirt and asphalt and freeways into a haze.
You know, it doesn't always end this way. Breakers
hurtling into those great, weathered cliffs, foam
left bubbling on the low rocks. Take the landscape
and its memories, coyotes yowling between
orange rock. Another moon, or the same one but from
another time, a different angle. Which is it that we want,
to remember, or to forget? Or is there a third option.
As if we can just come and go
sleeping on beaches, light breaking through fog.
The constantly shifting sand erasing
any sign we had been there, just like that.

[go to page 32]

You Were the Equator

You told me a story about my Antarctic feet
where I was a glacier
sliding over steaming green jungles like a
slow song.

You said
about my hips,
how they fit into your hands so specifically,
thumbs pressing down on me
and my lips parting like a sacred sea for you
right before the moment (or two, or three)
when I thawed into nerves
and syllables.

Lullaby

Her lips are on yours, those
gray surrendering skies.
Her fingers inch across you
like a slow moaning night train
from outside your third-story window,
and those moon eyes reach toward
                your lighthouse, her longing
                breaking a low haze.
                You imagine you can touch her
                strings, play her like a cello
                until her bones glow
                red hot through her skin
       until her love is
the pounding rain on ashes.

Topography is All Surface

A man with no arms or a man with no legs, which

would I rather? you're asking me

as I glance into the empty-black rearview mirror.

My tongue reaches to the broken flesh of my cheek. One car

alone on this two-lane stretch of highway.

I'm considering the role of hands, mostly the extent to which my hips

will remember

yours, absorbing each movement, as if you could sense our

impact on the molecules

like a series of waves on a graph, hard science.

Versus soft science. The memory

of delicate and slow, despite any other truth. I know you

used to study erogenous zones

referencing diagrams occasionally. A strategic move, no longer

a requisite

of love, but a life-sized game on opposite squares, knight moves in,

body of the queen against his body against the wall. Again.

Metal armor empty in a pile on the floor. Nonchalant? Not exactly.

The whole periphery edges in. An equinox

coming too fast, it's just beyond the tracks, Pacific Standard or so,

a mess

of fat Doug Firs resting there season after season. They get it,

topography is all surface,

but there are mountains somewhere below.

They feel it in their roots, slight vibrations from the dirt

like voices from another conversation fragmenting in and out.

And further south, Loja hummingbird—nectarivores,

their long tongues make it work, limbs or no limbs.

Our moonlight excursion to the swinging bridge

with a frayed rope and a coal black suture

to hold it all just so against the rock. Legs.

When I bite my cheek it's sex, not love, that taste of metal in my blood,

the same blood and metal of an old winter,

at a playground with a tongue stuck to a pole,

hopeful practice for a hopefully

intimate moment. Love wanting sex.

Not sex wanting love.

I snap my eyes open when the road blurs.

What else? The small life of a screech owl, monogamous

but it's complicated. Nothing to be concerned about, true monogamy

is hard,

maybe even too much for us

all of us.

Still, they know where home is, what it is.

Perhaps I could reach out further, hands grazing the froth of a wave

as it pulls away.

I don't have to decide, but it feels important, in this car,

speeding down a dark road

beside you, like the information will show up

someday, on legal documents or a résumé.

That's that, I say, No legs.

[go to page 71]

This is love, not geology

Starting on my lower lip
and spilling down
toward my ankles
you form a river
from the gloss of a
wet, blue marker

you travel upstream
with the marker between
your teeth
tracing tributaries
over my thighs
across sacral plexus

nerves slow-eroding
my cutaneous layer
until we become
a lake.

[go to page 35]

The Physical Things

1.

Redwoods trees, Paisano in the afternoon.
Holes in a blue dress. Blue dress hanging
on a doorknob. A sincere apology, to feel guilty,
not believing in unrequited love or ghosts
or the zodiac sky. Shark heart
served on a plate, peyote and square dancing
in an orange, dark place full of sand and adobe
and sunset.

2.

The moon enters the scene this way,
too small to cast much light. Two boys
walk down the ramp
toward the beach where our bodies lie,
bellies moving up and down in rhythm, it seems,
with the earth. I bet the boys could barely see
our skin, just silhouettes. They might have imagined
romance, only a fraction
of how love functions.
Us, we could blame it on
the shark we ate, an aphrodisiac or a predator
or just an animal acting like an animal. You
reach up my skirt as we drive
toward the beach. Before

the boys appear,
just the waves and a shard of moon:

the physical things come first. Spattered light
through a canopy of Redwood leaves, hard scratches
on our knees from the bark, a little blood shared between body
and body and earth. Or a bottle of coconut rum, a seedy
motel room near Puget Sound, bed sheets, the whitest white,
taken from the instant between dreaming and waking, color
of small deceptions, of truce, twisted around us.
Then, you on your way,
I on mine. Perhaps you feel sorry
with your bottle of rum,
your jug of Paisano, drawing the curtains
to block out the whole bright afternoon.
Instead of the alternative. The truth is
I wanted to live through it all at any cost,
another function of love. Perhaps the entrance point
is how the moon changes
the equilibrium of a room
as soon as we both come.

3.

We were talking about the future
in terms of cities. We wanted to swim
in the ocean at night. I wanted more.

Is this what happens when the moon appears
at the wrong time?

The boys want to build a fire where we are. They bring their dry wood.
But the ocean is gone, Big Sur and Coos Bay
are gone. Who's there? Who stands at the edge and looks up?

We like to hear the water when we fuck. We like to sit naked
under the moon. Yes, this is it. We are talking about places
with no names.

[go to page 41]

Suicide

What were you doing there
pinched hollow as a bullet hole

behind your grief, long willows dormant
and hushed in your head? On a tire swing

unspun like a dizzy child. Running from a monsoon overhead
out of breath and wet, girl, not so unlike the fitful orgasms

that would have had you yet. Or surrounded
by banks of sand and a white circle moon

night's translucence passing through your
ocean's hands. A burning kite chasing another

across an empty sky. If only twenty-six-year-old me
could have told fourteen-year-old you.

Highway songs up and down the Pacific coast
grabbing you and holding on

your lover dozing beside you until dark
sliding up from the water

covers the road's curves
drawing shadows across the dotted

lines. And you would have found a turn-out and slept
on his shoulder, beside a cliff, with the smell of sea

and night sinking back into its secret,
not leaping over the edge, not even thinking of it.

Safe

To be wild and unpretentious
to be both suspecting and unsuspecting
blue-ish light on our faces
from the moon
perhaps inside us
as well

And a fence that keeps children
from wandering off
that hides them
from the wilderness
and the wilderness
from them   the dusk sky
its size
sits at odds as barrier
and possibility

and the unknowns   the questions
thought up for the first time
of love and grief and death
and how to proceed still knowing
almost nothing
the far dark spaces
of ourselves

Today we keep breathing
as we believe we will
the flowers pressed between pages of

War and Peace
jars full of dusty pennies
waiting to be counted
and spent

or not waiting
at all
or they're waiting
but not for what we thought

Now here we are
on an empty beach
the dark clouds at a standstill
against the rising waves

Sometime before we realize what fear is
the ocean has lured us in
gasping with life

Home Remedies

Seasonal Affective Disorder: add rose petals to boiling water,
drink after cooling.

Dark circles under eyes: apply area with crushed mint leaves.

Insomnia: *cannabis indica*, smoked or ingested. Some for you and
some for your lover who is currently able to sleep just fine.

Solidarity must be the remedy for something.
And love. Or what feels like love.

For relief from topical habañero burn, smear with sour cream. And this
time he even took a picture to document the event. A close-up of your
face, nose centered, white spread thick from below your bloodshot,
burning eyes down to your chin.

Now you have: Consequences, for the record.
Note to self: do not re-title poem Placebos.

Even one-night stands can stand in: complex business of life,
check. More than just distraction, frustration, disease, discomfort,
disappointment. Afternoon rain tapping in libidinous rhythm. A tipsy
memory of rope and ice cube role-playing with a stranger, a good one.
We comb through, some don't slip through the teeth unnoticed: true.
Not like pink boxer-briefs that momentarily caught your attention,
more like the threesome with your best friend and a guy called Gomez.
He did her first, you remember? You remember, you made shadow
shapes on the wall with your idle fingers, check.

And what about today, since that was some years ago, you're thinking about the future too, when your now-lover moves on, finds himself a one-night stand to add to his collection of save-able experiences, good for him. But jealousy isn't so congratulatory. Today, he is on his way over to make love to you as the summer heat beats so libidinously against your skin and bones. In six months he'll have found the satin sheets of a mystery brunette seductress, his lips inching across her big breasts, sucking on her nipples. You and your heart, an arsenic pushing from inside. The subtle remnants of habañero on your fingers. Also, what he told you afterward as he rubbed himself against your sour cream face:

Hot peppers contain the main component of pepper spray, *Capsaicin*. He whispered that sexy word in your ear over and over like a hymn.

Psychologists say: ingest enough Capsaicin and your endorphins will kick in.

Endorphins can provide temporary relief from all sorts of ailments: loneliness, anxiety, lovesickness, controlled by the mess of circuits and wires and organs and blood that you are made of.

But sometimes: you have to sit on the beach in your jeans, this desperate edge of land, and let the rising tide wash over you, until it doesn't, falling back, and you are soaking wet, uncomfortable, choking on sea water. Sometimes the only remedy for suffering is suffering.

[go to page 7]

With Regard to Sunsets

At the edge of Browne's Addition
a cliff faces a creek and four arching bridges

the tallest an old train bridge that passes through a cluster of pines
before it shrinks into a speck. Trains that roar and squeal

shaking the ground, you and I, graduate students
on summer break, on magic mushrooms

there at the edge while the sun across the gorge
sets through the arch of a train bridge.

Your ugly white sunglasses passed back and forth
and this and us perhaps amidst *the best*

sunset ever, we say. Me laughing with you
on that cliff near an ordinary beautiful train bridge, long graffiti-

streaked train wobbling by, in Spokane, Washington, but I can't recall
how that sunset could have looked so different from others—

the one in Paris, on New Year's Eve,
from the fucking Eiffel Tower, flinging sparks

off the glossy metal right into the next year. Or the one that dove
slow motion into foam and waves as I drove down the coast

of Northern California. All the good ones are orange and yellow
and pink and the sun is a big flat golden circle on a big flat sky

and we feel infinite, or not, depending on if we remember to.
And then they disappear. It's like walking through an abstract

art exhibit trying to find meaning in the lines and colors of each
individual painting until you point at one, it is enormous,

and suddenly the polished floors and fluorescent lights dissolve.
You are standing in the painting, pointing at the outside world.

Two

Buenos Aires, 2011

When it rains and after, quiet
settles in pockets of shadows
between buildings.

A dragonfly in its impromptu dance
flitting into white and violet blossoms
that sit mute on the branches above.

Look, the haphazard
graffiti surfacing from beneath a layer
of white paint: *Que Dios nos ayude a todos.*
The river is close by,
warm and brown with sand
after so much wearing down.

Time implicit in rock, in bone,
in obscurity, a tumbleweed floating through
the space of a mind. I notice the music only

when it stops. And what about the dawn
as it climbs from the night and smog like wildfire
and stretches across the horizon,

that fire, what about it? It's true

the world could suddenly begin
to burn down, a spark catching the horizon,
and I'd be thinking of

how I had brushed my fingers over
the poem on your forearm, when I'd said,
tattoos are permanent, and you'd responded

are they? with our bare legs draped over the other's.
I read the words aloud
but I was thinking of what it means

to be *permanent*.
This city, its cracked cobblestone
and glass high-rises. Its traces

of stillness when bolts of translucent lightning
take off across the sky.
I don't notice what's missing

until a couple appears
in one of the hundreds of windows
dancing by candlelight, their soft silhouettes

floating beside them like the angels
of ghosts. I don't notice
until one day one of them

is gone,
the striking whiteout of uncertainty opening
like a heavy curtain.

[go to page 64]

28 Reasons to Set My Furniture on Fire

Bedbugs. Nightmares. New Age therapy for pyrophobia.

If the furnace died just after midnight, the snow angels covered
by more snow.

A rejection of Materialism. A mirror suddenly reversing the flow
of ancient rivers.

Fire can easily be waves of hypnosis

and dullness, a flat stretch of corn and clouds.

Perhaps, there is nothing else to do, no other heavy oak
erotic coffee table,
its sturdy legs never giving out.

Yes, I would light that table on fire.

And after driving all night throwing small things from the window

like the blue dress
and the blue curtains
and the blue glow of the bedroom
some sunny mornings,

all the spices on the spice rack, especially the cumin, and maps on the walls,
bus maps and walking tours from Austin, Amsterdam, Santiago, San Francisco, etc.

there was still so much more to lose.

The water was boiling.

The power went out.

We had nothing left to say.

I'd already tried everything else.

I followed a young girl as she snipped red dahlias from neighbors' gardens.

I walked, and walked

barefoot on the grass as a round moon moved across the night.

With a pocket knife I cut out a few dates on a calendar.

Some easy, contemporary voodoo.

All of it, burning the remnants and obscuring the old spaces.

Exothermalism,

the philosophy of leaving what's gone behind
through combustion.

I'd already tried everything else

like growing rosemary in the window sill

and stacking all the books against the door.

[go to page 37]

Math

1.

Start with a headcase, call her N lost
in a vast blue grid of equations: the square root
of X divided by the sum of its parts, bits of childhood
in there, bits of breakfast and love swirling like pheromones
on their carnal axis; X over (Y plus five) equals lust,
fixating on those surges of absurd
calculation as he considers her angles, isosceles
legs this way, more friction, try less, try falling
not like rain, but a leaf into his palms from a wide, unknown space;
X equals Y if Y could dismantle obstinate sound, an electric saw
with dull and missing teeth in the hands of a man
unable to discern branches dead
from alive until, finally, the green straw of life begins to show.
As if math could catalog and account for each
decision made, each emotion as it builds a wall around us
or passes through us like a ghost. Is the moon a variable,
triggering the water in our bodily oceans to shift,
the numbers to invert, new probabilities formed?
More importantly, are there any constants?

2.

Ellen and Steve's marriage, calculate based on the equation:
X equals sex over occupational frustration, variables to include
economic decline, the furnace going out, the fire.
Add Ellen's fear—certain men will inevitably leave their wives

for younger women. They don't all seem like bad men.
Or is it worse that they *aren't* all bad men.
Love, a bomb shelter under the plutonium plant.
It might begin with a receiver click after an almost silent breath,
then again, and again. Jealousy plus imagination,
a robin flies unknowingly into the bay window
and falls to the cold earth on its broken wing.
A headcase, the sum of her parts floating like pieces of an airplane
in the sea, unaccounted for?

3.

These algorithms have rules, a finite number of steps
that should solve any problem, but every sequence
has infinite possibilities. Cut deep into limestone, the bomb shelter
no one ever found. Was it too obvious or not obvious enough?
My father says, do not spend money on the dead,
a practical rule. Ask someone else,
and they've planted yellow rosebushes around their lover's grave
which they pay groundskeepers to maintain
for any number of reasons, infinite possibilities within
other infinities. Equations without answers.
Perhaps mourning is less exhausting
if we have something else. A yellow rosebush,
or a small clay jar, ashes wheeling down a cliff
into the sea where breakers splash hard against the rocks,
or those ashes diluted in a watering can and poured
into peace lilies by the window.

4.

Here's a true story. A boy wakes his girlfriend about a dream
in which she cuts her *long, beautiful hair*—he actually calls it
a *nightmare*—and he's sitting in the great pile of it on the floor, his sobs
echoing across the bright white space
of his imaginary emptiness, in this case, a colossal unfurnished room.
Then he says, my love *is* conditional, stroking her hair
as the girl turns away from him, pretending to sleep.

[go to page 59]

We find an empty part of the river

brown at its wide mouth
far enough that the bongo drummers
and tambourine players

won't bother to see
beneath the copper sunset
lovers bobbing with soft waves

gulping in air between mouths
full of the other
      and afterward

      what remains will open like moonlight
      over the water   like the strange
      shapes of desire and distance

      ships ablaze at sea
      the blur of molecules around that fire
      and the jumping shadows on the water's surface

      or perhaps left over will be nothing more
      than a quick coalescence of chemicals
            and whatever else has loosened from us

like ghosts hungry for abandon
will wash to shore nameless
with the fractured husks and bones

of fish dead a thousand years
learning the depths of other
lonelier darknesses.

Suspension

He's either chopping leeks—and I've only noticed just now how his hands are smooth, no cuts—or he's brushing loose strands of hair from my face while I am slumped next to the counter. We look up to snow piling on the window sill, glinting under muted street lights. Or maybe we go to the Hanging Gardens of Babylon, he holds his hand up in the green iridescence to the moon, so huge and round and near. Held by strings, the whole place swings like a footbridge crossing through giant wet leaves, fat vines looping over a gully far below. Of course with a sharp knife he could slash those strings with one swipe, but he's too careful to let it slip, and he thought he was still crouched on the floor with me, why would he bring the knife? Perhaps he wants us to feel sudden, weightless for the instant before we admit that sometimes love also dies. Yes I know, even from this kitchen, there is a fall.

[go to page 50]

This is geology, not love

that we've been talking about.
Why is your igneous in my

esophagus, and where are your fault lines
hiding in safety under the tide

until it falls away? Or maybe magma
pumps hot through the veins

of our house, a clever form of love
making. If it is hypothetical

maybes we're after, maybe a river
ran through my spleen, deposited you instead

of sediment. Tectonics between us
are convergent these days,

you live in my lithosphere
I live in your trench. We're not

vibrating on impact, our earth
emerging up, up, clean

and unmarked and given important names
like Himalaya or Appalachian. Instead,

we buckle over
each other. We used to care

about topography—exploring
you ran

your hands across the skin
delicately hiding the ribcage

of Wyoming, unconcerned by the sleeping
catastrophe beneath. But this is fucking

geology: erosion
and rock cycles. Hot spots

include Hawaii and Iceland
in addition to Wyoming—

not my vagina, especially not
my heart. Ring of Fire means

the Pacific Rim, twenty-five thousand
miles of ruthless earthquakes

and volcanoes
that have destroyed cities, whole islands,

killed and killed and killed,
a direct result

of plate tectonics, not love, not even
what happens after. To be fair,

acts of nature don't have will, can't
truly be ruthless.

[go to page 8]

Pier 26 at Half Moon Bay

The sea says go
    go?
    Which way to home,
    to nostalgia?

    Those bodies with long shadows
shrink at the vanishing point.
That illusion.

Have I been here before
in the cold walking to my car
    shivering

the car, a greenhouse
filthy windows

as I sit in the driver's seat
and shut the door
sun-warmth filling in

    and for a moment
I am without others, without other
moments   as if

through Cambria and Cretacea

all this time

shells left under the earth
like breadcrumbs
have led to this effortless place.

See the old lighthouse from the pier,
green light flashing, go, go, go? Waves underneath
hurtle into the pillars, a language

of rolling echoes.   This museum
of looking back.

I should protest when they lift me,
carry me away. Nostalgia, lighthouse,

the vanishing point, or is it me,
a diminishing speck?
    It isn't.

I am alone on a pier. I am in my car. The sun is straight ahead,
bright crystalline streaks across my vision.

[go to page 20]

The House of Sixteen Doors

The cockroaches come, wriggling out
of drains, searching for sugar

in droplets of Malbec between the kitchen
and garden. We are on Neruda's terrace

and he is reading his poems. Reading them into
the sky, the flora, the stone floor, and all of these

eternities we dream up. Half-hidden
in the shade of drooping vines, the black dog sleeps.

Like omens, buses screech to hard halts,
like poems and dreams, I know, Neruda says,

of love that is slow and difficult. Isles where
we will wait awhile, but

we don't know what we're waiting for.
His house has sixteen doors, I've counted.

Winds blow, doors slam,
that omen

reaching out past the shadows
of shadows. The dog scrambles behind me.

Noise and silence press against
the other like young lovers

still unable to name their fear.
In the aftermath

majesty palms and jasmine vines
blooming summer solstice

on the opposite hemisphere
as if to search into another world

for answers
or questions

we walk through the house
wondering

if all the doors
have already slammed shut.

What Was Left

*Since [the Golden Gate Bridge] opened on
May 27, 1937, there have been an estimated
1,600 deaths in which the body was recovered, and many more unconfirmed.*
– LA Times

I stood over a porcupine, crushed beneath a rock,
its blood still warm, pooling on the gravel.
Blood like that, wet,

would well up in carpet and also drip down walls,
blood like adhesive to bits of bone
left hanging like ornaments. A shot would strike

like chalk-hot thunder, long
and slow
like summer solstice, like the grave

of summer solstice at the end
of a long barrel. Now,
I remember the smell of cordite.

A young girl in Milwaukee, Wisconsin wants to die.
Perhaps she could take a Greyhound bus
across the Great Plains and Rockies

and Sierras, reaching the bridge too late,
she'd change her mind, she wouldn't quite know why,
seeing mountains for the first time from the huge

bus windows, she'd want to get out and touch them. Although
she didn't go to San Francisco. That hazy Impressionistic sunset
dropped into the bay without her. She stayed home

and grabbed her stepfather's shotgun from the wall,
her shoulders slumped, sad moon eyes
squeezed shut as she pulled the trigger.

And now the porcupine is curling itself up tight,
shaking. It shoots spines into my dog's mouth,
her cheek, so close to her eyes,

and my throat is filling, as if I'm held
underwater. Impervious, she refuses to retreat,
quills amassing on her face. I know about fight-or-flight, fear

ascending from the stomach, like a phone call
from one girl to another,
her parents choking on sobs, and me sinking

beyond the white linoleum of my family's kitchen floor.
I would hardly call it a fight, really, just a sudden
calm, awful silence erupted. The spiny ball limp on the dirt,

half beneath a heavy rock I found somewhere nearby.
No misty spirit floated up from
what was left

as I had always wanted to believe it did
from Nicole's body, a deep-rooted ritual
of something more. Only this absence

of sound. This.

[go to page 60]

The Midwest

We would play *MacGyver* near the water,
McKinley Marina, nightfall, a cord wrapped around my legs
where you let the skin rub away,
a little blood to convince us of our danger,
our wilderness
before you'd kiss me, tied up, kiss me, released.

This scar near my left ankle a kind of dark passage.

Beside us Lake Michigan stretched in quiet nakedness
beyond the passing boats.

So,
I have another scar on my right wrist from a small pit viper.
A kayak in the leafy rainforest.
A beautiful Bolivian sucking at the base of my hand,
her full brown lips pressed against me so seriously.
Bright green birds, their voices ricocheting between Ceiba trees.

It reminded me of vertigo, drifting, drifting until a new

unfamiliar world would appear.

A third scar centered on my left foot is an escape wound.
Low stuttering, thunder's ascent from a frozen lake.
Jagged fragment of ice, then crystals of blood
glittering up to the great northern night sky

where aurora borealis feels close to dying

to living

the water's far dark edge right up to the sky's.

The truth is
not all of this is true.
And there are other lies too.
I'm sorry.

The truth has been tougher to track down.

You drew a thick outline of Wisconsin behind my left shoulder
with the words *where go the boats* written inside.
Lake Michigan invisible to the east.
It's all invisible now
but I can still run over it with my hands.

Buenos Aires, 2011

1.

To hide in a city—smokestack sky
and old billboards, narrow orange roads
unnamed. We can hide from
ourselves, and northern winter
nothing but a cerebral trick, the fire
of sunset drifting through
specks of snowfall. He says to me,
Jessica, I don't love you, cupping my face
and kissing me. Why?
If only we were less like us, more
like Borges' cats, living each instant
as its own eternal world.
I see the open space of his sidelong gaze
toward the window, white of his eyes, sheer
curtains half-closed. As if time is trying
to drop out from under us,
and in that first cognizance
of falling, we are lovers again. On the roof,
I would lie my head in his lap and he'd rest
his hands on my chest. The heartsickness,
the tiredness in us.

2.

A window opens and someone
throws a bag of trash
onto the street. A window opens
and a cat's face appears.
A window opens and the city is
a cautious static
of heat and smog. Perhaps I'm sick
of truth, too, the out-of-sightness,
I know we can't keep on this way.
From the roof I see a building
dirty and colorless except for the top floor,
which is burnt yellow, its cement crumbling,
its terrace holding a small garden,
hanging vines. It seems dreamlike.
Is it? Inside, someone is
boiling their lentils, scrubbing
their clothes on an old washboard
until the skin on their fingers
cracks from soap and bleach, before
hanging them out to dry.
And there goes the cat, zigzagging
through the flapping bed sheets and blouses,
back and forth.

Three

An Incomplete List of Everything

Quiet olfactory of winter, snow
or no snow. Mount Spokane.
Where the glaciers have stopped. Where they still shift
without notice. A preference not to know.
A steamer and its thick trail of smoke
disappearing into the isthmus. Hibiscus
in violet and red. Melancholy. Morning, long shadows
of mountains over the beach. A dog in the window,
sensing the hills pulsing before a storm.
Redwoods, even Pines. Traveling south
along the coast, south until
we recognize nothing. Cow heart on the menu.
One mosquito net for both of us
to sleep beneath. Sex. Flash
of equinox moon on the water, paper boats
sailing through pond grass, you said
it reminded you of soft music,
the thrush, then silence. Constellations
like distant cityscape. The wilderness of lust.
Desert plains sprinkled with blue
wildflowers. Swarming horseflies sticking
to droplets of half-evaporated sweat.
Lightning snaps over a barren field, someone
is there, looking straight up. The unspeakable things,
whether or not it was love, skeptical
of nostalgia. Hard like bleach. Kerosene,

flames. Bright orange dusk across the coast, hidden
rocky cove, one dead seal sparkling in sea foam.
To see the white moon rise
and fall. Forgiveness. And there is hugeness, too,
and distance is a factor. And what is not real.
Cliffs, bones hanging from a Joshua tree.
Seismic energy, San Andreas Fault,
faults in general. And blame.
A bedroom, scissors on the dresser,
shiny blades reflecting worried eyes,
body parts stretching and collapsing on
themselves. Silence after a blizzard,
dress hanging on the doorknob
the morning after.

Elk Public House, 1:37am

Before I can think about it, or
yes this is the way a body thinks

after a few beers, you have me pressed
against the sink, you have my jeans at my ankles, lost

and light in this suddenly
open field, its cool night falling to my

bare shoulders, and some distant birds
with beautiful voices, they're singing

through the walls of buzzing electronica
stripping the filth from the mirror,

all anatomy in permanent marker
labeled with fat black arrows:

cunt, *balls*, and *fuck me*
if you're in the (area code) *509*

melting away like sound muffled underwater
now in this dark field

of grass and stars, yes
keep ignoring the banging on the door

this urgency of being
here, now

barely undressed, this urgency,
you looking at me

the way we watch a fire
burn down a forest.

OkCupid

Hi. My name is Jessica. I am twenty-six years old. I have lived in eight cities and all of their cobbled alleys, dingy subway stairwells I know by heart. I'm telling you this because I would like you to make assumptions about me. The picture you see, it's me holding that baby lion cub, on the outskirts of Buenos Aires. This is meant to intrigue you, a young girl holding a wild animal. I believe in feng shui. I am a poet. I'd be impressed if you'd read poetry with me. If you were able to talk about the future with both gravity and ease. A ninety-eight percent match. Is this destroying the mystery, the magic? I'm asking you. And I'm asking myself. Love is like an algorithm. Parallel answers to survey questions could lead to lust then love then that's it, so easy, easy as atoms attracting and repelling each other. Based on laws that simply exist. Laws that are us. I should mention that I may have a complex. About language. About commitment. About what love is exactly. If you bring me to the highest spot in the city, where we can hear ourselves echoing through the hills, Mount Hood sitting ghostlike in the misty distance, I'll want to mistake that expansiveness in every direction for a spark. But try describing a scent, let's say the ocean, with something better than *ocean*. Brief winter sun of the far north shimmering against the icicles, the sound of cold, somewhere we're waking from it. I know what's true. No one's wandering into my room while I'm alone with a book or a movie or empty brown beer bottles piling up on the nightstand; no one's barging in unless I set my house on fire.

[go to page 29]

Research

Worms rise from the dirt after hot rain
near Cody, Wyoming at eight-thousand feet,
mountain air still wet as storm clouds split—
the sky appears. Me, wearing a blue dress,
in tall switch grass
akin to the wind. Perhaps if I close my eyes,
scent of worms,
wild mushrooms crushed in my fist.
Long ago, painted turtle
from a nearby pond, by my hands,
in my home. I had to go back
and let him go when my mother said
he would die if I kept him. I was miserable.
On the mountain, sun
forcing a ribbon of light across my face.
Maybe that is all the transparency we get.

Craving a Burrito at a Market, San Telmo, Buenos Aires

Fresh earth sticks to the edges of lettuce
and onion roots, the scent dispersed
into the air, dregs of wilderness still clinging
as I scan the shelves—dozens of eggs wrapped
in beige paper, table salt, rock salt, iodized, kosher,
coarse, and sea salt, a wall filled
with bottles of red wine.
But no black pepper, no pinto beans, no tortillas.
My grocery list is useless.

The produce man is hiding
among crates of apples
and celery as I wait, arms full of Malbec
instead of food. His drowsy,
hazel eyes magnetic
like a mystic's, like he can stir the earth
spirit that sleeps in the vegetables.
The man smiles, hears the Wisconsin
in my words as I ask for *albahaca*,
but he's already drifted somewhere
else, back to a Bolivian summer—
a tattered soccer ball ricochets
off the walls of abandoned buildings
on a narrow street, dust

kicked up into a lucent film
just before the sun slumps behind the city,
orange, then gray. I smile back,

the spark from his dreaming
a brief portal to wherever he is.
A box of ripe avocados sits on the floor,
but I'm no longer envisioning a fat burrito stuffed
with beans and rice and guacamole. The romance
is over, but the man is still smiling at me,
holding out a hand
with my *albahaca*, which I will keep in a jar
of water on the window sill. In December,
warm winds from the river
will ripple in, albahaca in the wet air
unfolding its verdant stench.

Dear Mike Polansky,

One great body of water. Nowhere to land. As if the oceans swallowed it up. An iceberg on which I'd been floating. Empty sea to empty sea.

Then there we were, strangers. In a strange city, a wedding, a surplus of ceremonial magic amassing between us in the mess of hearts and bodies.

I wonder what it's like to find meaning in coincidences. To be the one who maps them out. Some could be valleys, some archipelagos, some cities on islands, some cities lost.

You grabbed the book from my hands, read the final page to me. A makeshift-keepsake-bookmark, an old San Francisco bus transfer fell out, drifted like my heart's last feather to the floor. I could have gone back to last year. With him, up to my chin in precipitous hills. Western glow of fog sitting midair. But I left it.

Perhaps it's just a concept being brought to life. The lovely chaos of beginning again. I barely knew you, but in your hands you held a small fire which you gave to me. If your experience differed from mine, don't worry. How we feel has little to do with reciprocity, and this is good. I only want to thank you.

With love,
Jessica

[go to page 12]

Chemistry on Hold

Bread in its bag, day-old

baby blue speckled like snow
across a field of wheat

sticking to the tips only

the Great Plains and the great

loneliness

of such a space, vast and flat

this stillness, this morphing from life

to shelf life.

Once, I was without
this conundrum of memory
of our lower halves

hands holding my hips in that flowery dress

drinking barley wine in a hotel room

shades of mauve

and time drifting mauve to

gray, this precision of colors

that precede disaster, the sky

of a few twisters
of a wheat field
and afterward

that rain being cold, dress dripping heavy
onto concrete steps.

And, since the beginning, roots uprooting,
sycamore
young, climbing through shallow dirt. My sky so distant
a blue, the spark a cross-handling of cables, dusk fire sitting like fog

like us in our twenties at nightfall on a terrace
in Buenos Aires. Darkness a shield, you behind it
with another girl singing our favorite songs
like they were only songs.
Children in the narrow streets
squealing like bats, splitting the night into crystals.

We see our reflections

only our former selves instead

only the dog tired and smiling on a cold marble floor.

Now, who is dreaming? Who is lost
with us, dreaming, waiting
to dream or to lose,
one body in the quiet plains,
for how long?

A loose wire dangling from a pole, half disconnected.
The wind, dangerous as fire, dangerous with fire.

Love isn't a word, *I know*, but
is this true?

Is this true? What am I saying

I can live with

or without?

Interrupted by the Infinite, in a Field or a Train or a Dream or

I. Morning

From here, I can see the whole beach
curving around the bend, all beige
and glittering Mediterranean blue.
And I can see a few nearby
pueblos scattered inland,
houses like broken teeth
risen from the earth.

I see a rock jutting out of the sea.

In legend, in a time of great love
and great power and
overhauling loss,
this rock is the heart's notch
missing from the western ridge
of the mountain
right where I'm standing.

II. Untitled

A long sigh, its heat
rising to
the weight of his sleep
he wraps around me.
Illusion, night, waking.
At any moment
he might pull me
right through him.

III. Morning

A spoon scrapes pulp from a grapefruit.
I don't love you.
Flowers breathe,
Gold Hibiscus in thick
jungles. I don't love you. Whispery,
humid I don't love you's. The spoon, the fruit,
the flowers, they notice it?
Are they listening
and if they are   what,
what then?

IV. Part One

Memory, I wait by the shore.

Tiny rocks digging into my feet.

A dream drums beneath the water.

V. Dear Body,

It was then I jumped from the boat. Into the ocean. I climbed back up, and I jumped again. The warm water and the big sun. Hear me out. A partial absence. I leapt from the boat? Dear body, whom I have affronted. Dear body, you might be all I have. Please forgive me this trespass, body, body of water, ocean. Please forgive me this. For the land, and the landslides, the disasters. I was lost. The truth, yes, I am. We have never been indestructible, I know. I will listen. Now you are wavering. Now you are scared. Body as life. Body as prayer. Dear body, I am here now.

VI. Part Six

Elephant sleep cycles: thirty minutes at a time.

The origin of lipstick: In Mesopotamia women smearing semi-precious jewels onto their mouths.

Taxonomy of lightning bugs: *Photuris lucicrescens*

Pause to chop this up
                              for a dream.

VII. The Distant Past

We were inside the afternoon,
imagining a rainstorm, quick
and dark moving across the sun,

picking up every toy in the yard,
wind sharp and whipping our long brown hair
over our faces.

[go to page 27]

The Graveyard's in the Backyard, Where the Meadow Used to Be

Last night when I was young I saw a man looking at me.

Sometime before the blue dark oceans rose
our mouths hushed by water when we tried to speak.

I saw weeds accumulating in the backyard
and never thought to do anything.

Last night before I helped that man with a flat tire

I never thought to question.

I only gave him a bunch of money and no,
he didn't have a gun.

Lucky, I guess.

Sometime, anytime, before blowing crack smoke
onto a crack-head's dick.

When all the men in the world were looking at me.

When I'd feign shyness and lower my eyes coyly.

There's another look too
that came later.

A locking gaze
pouted lips and all.

A lover, The Lover. Perhaps

where passion became Passion.

Shade, willow tree, a place to hide, hands grabbing
all hot afternoon.

How the sun never let up, never moved,
the way the sun never moves. We could learn

to imitate science, couldn't we?

A peaceful black dog asleep on my feet,
her sigh rises and falls beneath her chest.

We could learn
how to build bridges that last forever
ish.

Contributors:

Jessica Lynch designed the cover, assisted with book layout, and provided emotional support and light through the latter end of the emotional turmoil, recovery, and growth that led to the creation of many of these poems. She is also the exclusive designer of my websites, and co-owner of Jessica & Jessica LLC.

Omar Cabrales Terrazas is the musician behind the custom-made soundtracks that accompany this book. He has also provided endless support in the making of the physical book, constantly adding to the beautiful machine of ideas that propel forward my ability to create in uncountable ways.

Eilish Connor is the artist behind the custom-made artwork that adorns the front and back of this book. Her enthusiasm and precision in conveying what lies in these pages visually showcase her talent and depth of consciousness. She was also a pillar of support during the end of the story told here, sharing warmth and wisdom when it was most needed.

Brandon Getz is the primary inspirator and editor of the poems in this book. Despite the roughness that accompanied our strange and marvelous relationship, he is now not only a source of professional support, but a friend for life, which goes to show that the heart might well be loveliest without the ego.

I am infinitely grateful to have each of these people on my team.

Acknowledgements:

I would also like to extend a gigantic thank you to my family, the Lakritz clan. To my parents, Sheldon and Shirley, my sisters, Robin and Ali, and my brother Jake, for supporting my wayward ways without (much) question, and for true, unconditional love, which can't be underestimated. Extra, extra thanks to Jaime R Wood, Lillian Lakritz, Christopher Howell, and Eder Candido Zapata for their support in both professional and personal ways through the making of this book.

Grateful acknowledgement is made to the following publications where these poems or earlier versions of them first appeared:

Cream City Review: "This is love, not geology"
Touchstone: "Seventeen Reasons to Set My Furniture on Fire"
Sierra Nevada Review: "Craving a Burrito at a Market, San Telmo, Buenos Aires"
Thin Air Magazine: "This is geology, not love"
Third Coast: "An Incomplete List of Everything"
Pif Magazine: "We find an empty part of the river"
Five Quarterly: "The Physical Things"
Outside In: "The House of Sixteen Doors"
Ilanot Review: "Home Remedies"
Josephine Quarterly: "A Different Angle"
Penduline Press: "Elk Public House, 1:37AM" and "Suicide"
Grist: "Chemistry on Hold"
Glassworks: "The Graveyard's in the Backyard, Where the Meadow Used to Be"
Sweet Lit: "Dear Mike Polansky"
Squalorly Lit: "Buenos Aires, 2011"

To my amazing Kickstarter Backers: thank you for believing in me. Your generosity is forever imprinted.

Ade
Allmyfrnds
Amy K Greene (AML)
Amy Soderlund
Andrew Kaufman
Angie & Erich Roush
Ashley Wurzbacher
Beardaze - Mike & Kayla
Becky Thomas
Ben & Dani
Benjamin Máté
Breezie Aguirre
Brendan Lynaugh
Bruno Tereso
Bryce
Caren Shele Honigsfeld
César Perez-Ribas
Christian Lennartsson
Cliffe Connor
Daniel Bauke
Diana Sanchez
Domen Lavric
Dorothea Linnæus
Eddie Freeman
Edwin Ihlenfeld
Elizabeth Andrews
Erin Perkins
Gary Lakritz
Greg Leunig

Heather Johnson
Howie Lakritz
Jamaal Kraima
Jayne Geller
jo
Ken Lakritz
Kevin Veitia
Kevin Zoeteman
Kyrie Melnyck
Leif Hynnekleiv, MD
Liz Rognes
Mandy Iverson
Mariana Gonzalez
Mary McGregor
Meg Cassidy
Melissa Wong
Michael Zhang
Mike Hromada
MJ Bavaret
Natalie Lakritz & Sean Korb
Nick Papadakis
Nina Jarrah
Olivia M Croom
Pat English
Patrick Hargon
Richard Bartoshevich
Rob Malone
Ron Salamander
Ryan Schneider
Salma Saab
Sam Sielen
Samantha Kempen

Santiago Arvizu
Sarah A Manthe
Scott A Michel
Scott Horvitz
Steve Wood
Summer
Susanna Linnæus
Sven Schulz
Tito Bohrt
Tom Cincotta
Toma Tatuaje
Tyler Jackson
Tyler Patterson
Vijay Raj
Zac Witte
Zsolt Olah

Notes:

The dual structure of this book was inspired by Julio Cortázar's novel *Hopscotch*.

"28 Reasons to Set My Furniture on Fire" was inspired by a line from Adrienne Rich's poem "Victory."

"The House of Sixteen Doors" alludes to Pablo Neruda's poem "If You Forget Me."

"The Midwest" alludes to Louis Jenkins' poem "Where Go The Boats."

The allusion from "Buenos Aires, 2011" on p. 62 is from Jorge Luis Borges' short story "The South."

The poem titled "The Graveyard's in the Backyard, Where the Meadow Used to Be" is a line from the CocoRosie song "R.I.P. Burn Face," which inspired its creation.

www.ingramcontent.com/pod-product-compliance
Lightning Source LLC
Chambersburg PA
CBHW022228010526
44113CB00033B/740